An Awesome Siblingship of

__________  __________

Written by

____

Table of Contents

Foreword 3

Chapter 1 - The First Time We Met 5

Chapter 2 - You In My Eyes 8

Chapter 3 - My Best Memories Of Us 10

Chapter 4 - 30 Reasons Why You Are An Awesome Sibling 21

Chapter 5 - I'm Grateful For You 52

Chapter 6 - Photo Memories 54

Chapter Infinity 65

Foreword

Siblings:

Your only enemy you can't live without.

Chapter 1

The First Time We Met

The first time we met was the day

____

____

____

Although I don't remember much, but I knew that

____

____

____

____

____

____

Back then, I was ____(age) and you were ____(age)

When we met, I

because

Siblings:
Children of the same parents, each of whom is perfectly normal until they get together.

Chapter 2

You In My Eyes

Five words or phrases that come to my mind when I think of you:

1. ______________________________

2. ______________________________

3. ______________________________

4. ______________________________

5. ______________________________

Because I have a sibling, I'll always have a friend.

Chapter 3

My Best Memories Of Us

Of the many embarrassing things we have done together, this one stands out in my mind the most:

I remember when I was

One of my favorite fun times with you was

Do you remember when

I will never forget how funny it was when

I will never forget the moment of us when

I still can't believe that you

I remember

On my ______________________________, I remember that

____

____

____

____

____

____

____

____

____

____

____

____

____

____

I am sorry that

No matter what happens...
Some memories can never be replaced.

Chapter 4

30 Reasons Why You Are An Awesome Sibling

1. I like your

____

2. You are my favorite

______________________________ in the world

3. I like hearing stories about your

____

4. I like how talented you are at

____

5. I like to watch you

____

6. You definitely deserve the

__________________________________award

7. You have the greatest taste in

____

8. You make me want to be a better

____

9. I love to

______________________________________with you

10. I believe the world needs your unique ______________________________

11. I am so glad that you like my

____

12. It is so funny when you

____

13. I like it when you

____

14. I never get tired of your

____

15. I love how you never get tired of my

____

16. I like it when you wear

____

17. I am kind of obsessed with your

____

18. I like how you

________________________________everyday

19. I like how you

---

20. You know exactly what

____

21. I know that

____

22. You are

____

23. I can tell

____

24. You give the best

____

25. You're the only person in the world

who________________________________

26. Just by looking at you I

____

27. It's the worst when

____

28. You understand

____

29. You never

___

30. Together, we would be

____

I like you, because you join in on my
weirdness.

Chapter 5

I'm Grateful For You

Everyday, I am grateful that you

I'm so thankful for the moments.
So glad I got to know you.

Chapter 6
Photo Memories

These are some of my favorite photo memories of us together ☺

Insert
Photo
Here

Insert
Photo
Here

Insert
Photo
Here

Insert
Photo
Here

Insert Photo Here

Insert
Photo
Here

Insert
Photo
Here

Insert
Photo
Here

Insert
Photo
Here

I love those random memories that make me smile no matter what is going on in my life right now.

Chapter Infinity

Because of you, I had an amazing childhood that I will never forget.

Don't get one of those lame greeting cards from a store that will likely get lost after awhile. Get your loved ones something more meaningful that will put a smile on their faces every single time!

www.loveydoveygifts.com

Made in the USA
Las Vegas, NV
17 December 2025